An Audiobook

THE STORY OF MY EXPERIMENTS WITH TRUTH

autobiography - m. k. gandhi

Charkha audiobooks
where words find voice
An imprint of Karadi Tales Company Pvt. Ltd.

Voices	:	Shekhar Kapur as M. K. Gandhi
		Nandita Das as Narrator
Text Adaptation:		Anushka Ravishankar, Shobha Viswanath
Art	:	Thota Tharrani
Music	:	3 Brothers & A Violin
Design	:	Ansad

Published by
Charkha Audiobooks
an imprint of
Karadi Tales Company Pvt. Ltd.
3A Dev Regency 11 First Main Road Gandhinagar Adyar Chennai 600020.
Ph: 91 44 4205 4243 Fax: 91 44 2440 3728
Email: contact@karaditales.com
Website: www.karaditales.com

This Abridged Audiobook of
The Story of My Experiments with Truth
has been produced in 2005 by arrangement with
Navajivan Trust

ISBN 81-8190-059-6

Tenth Reprint 2013

Printed at
Indigo Press Byculla Mumbai 400027.

Publisher's Note

To abridge *The Story of My Experiments with Truth,* Gandhiji's autobiography, seemed in the beginning, like sacrilege. How could one abridge the life of the Mahatma?

But in a world that is increasingly moving away from the Mahatma and his ideals, Einstein's words seem prophetic. "Generations to come will scarcely believe that such a one as this, ever in flesh and blood, walked upon this earth." To that extent, even an abridged account of Bapu's life, we hope, is an inspiration.

We present this audiobook not so much as a reference to Gandhiji, but as an attempt to communicate the spirit of his life. If this audiobook inspires the listener-reader to seek to know more about Gandhiji's values, philosophy or life, this audiobook would have achieved its objective.

Most of the songs in this audiobook are among Gandhiji's favourites and find their context within the chapters.

We are grateful to Navajivan Trust for their spontaneous and unconditional support in the making of this audiobook.

Prologue

It was Friday, the 30th of January, 1948. The time was ten minutes past five in the evening.

Bapu was late for his prayer meeting. Supported on either side by his grand-nieces, Abha and Manu, he hurriedly climbed the steps up to the prayer ground. About five hundred people had gathered and were waiting to catch a glimpse of the Mahatma. Some moved towards him to touch his feet. Gandhi lifted his arms off the shoulders of Abha and Manu and stood for a moment, smiling, touching his palms together.

Suddenly, a man jostled his way out of the crowd. Manu thought he was trying to prostrate himself before Bapu, and she put out a hand to stop him. He hurled her out of the way, and standing about two feet in front of Gandhi, fired three shots at him.

When the first bullet struck, Gandhi's foot, which was mid-air, came down to the ground, but he remained standing. When the second bullet struck, the blood began to spread on Gandhi's white clothes.

"Hey, Ram!" he murmured.

Then the third bullet struck, and Gandhi's limp body fell lifeless to the ground.

Bapu was no more.

Mat jaa, mat jaa, mat jaa, jogi
Paav padhun main tere, jogi
Hindi Bhajan – Traditional

Do not go, do not go, do not leave, O saint
I fall at your feet, do not go, O saint

Introduction

It is not my purpose to attempt a real autobiography. I simply want to tell the story of my numerous experiments with truth, and as my life consists of nothing but these experiments, it is true that the story will take the shape of an autobiography.

I believe that a connected account of all these experiments will not be without benefit to the reader. My experiments in the political field are now known, not only in India, but also to a certain extent to the world. For me they are not of much value, and the title of 'Mahatma' that they have bestowed upon me has therefore even less. Often the title has deeply pained me.

The experiments that I am about to relate are spiritual. It is from these that I have derived the power that I possess for working in the political field. I am neither going to conceal nor understate any ugly things that must be told. I hope to acquaint the reader fully with all my faults and errors. My purpose is to describe my experiments in the science of Satyagraha, not to say how good I am.

I have given these reminiscences the title, **The Story of My Experiments with Truth.** *For me, truth is the sovereign principle, which includes numerous other principles. This truth is not only truthfulness in word, but truthfulness in thought also, and not only the relative truth of our conception, but also the Absolute Truth. There are innumerable definitions of God. But I see God as Truth only.*

The Ashram, Sabarmati
26th of November, 1925

1

The house of the Dewans of Rajkot stands as it stood a hundred and forty one years ago, in the little seaside town of Porbandar. On the 2nd of October 1869, in this large house, Putlibai, wife of the Dewan Karamchand Gandhi, gave birth to her youngest child. He was named Mohandas. It was the end of the nineteenth century, and the British Empire was at the peak of its wealth and power. India was in her second century of British domination.

No special celestial arrangement marked the arrival of Mohandas Karamchand Gandhi. No astrologer predicted the greatness that lay in store for this child. No seer divined that he would become one of the greatest apostles of non-violence, a man who would invoke the nobility of the human spirit, and become the father of a nation. No prophet foretold the birth of a Mahatma.

Along with two brothers and a sister, Mohandas spent some of his school years in Porbandar. Others were spent in the neighbouring dusty city of Rajkot.

I recollect having been put to school. It was with some difficulty that I got through the multiplication tables. The fact that I recall nothing more of my school days than having learnt to call our teachers all kinds of names, would strongly suggest that my intellect must have been sluggish and my memory raw.

I used to be very shy and avoided all company. My books and my lessons were my sole companions. To be at school at the stroke of the hour and to run back home as soon as the school closed, that was my daily habit. I could not bear to talk to anybody. I was also afraid lest anyone should poke fun at me.

This shy and awkward child was however, unusual in many ways. He never lied; refused to cheat; was unfailingly punctual, and had a blind and unquestioning respect for his elders.

In high school, Gandhi, who was frail and small-built, envied Sheikh Mehtab, a boy who often boasted to young Mohandas that he owed his strength and athletic abilities to the fact that he ate meat.

My friend's exploits cast a spell over me. He could run long distances and extraordinarily fast. He was adept in high and long jumping. He could put up with any amount of corporal punishment. I wanted to be like him. I could hardly jump or run. Why should I not be as strong as he?

Moreover, I was a coward. I used to be haunted by the fear of ghosts, thieves and serpents. I did not dare to stir out of doors at night. Darkness was a terror to me. It was almost impossible for me to sleep in the dark as I would imagine ghosts coming from one direction, thieves from another, and serpents from a third. My friend knew of all my weaknesses. He would tell me that he could hold in his hand live serpents, could defy thieves and did not believe in ghosts. And all of this was, of course, the result of eating meat.

A doggerel was in vogue amongst us at that time:

Behold the mighty Englishman
He rules the Indian small
Because being a meat eater
He is five cubits tall.

All this had its due effect on me. I was convinced that if the whole country took to meat eating, the English could be overcome.

A day was thereupon fixed for beginning the experiment. We went in search of a lonely spot on the river, and there I saw for the first time in my life – meat. The goat's meat was as tough as leather. I simply could not eat it. A horrible nightmare haunted me. Every time I dropped off to sleep it would seem as though a live goat was bleating inside me, and I would jump up full of remorse.

Despite the "live bleating goat" inside him, and the fact that he came from an orthodox vegetarian family, Gandhi took to eating meat clandestinely. However, this deception weighed heavily on him. He knew that every time he ate meat, he broke an implicit promise to his parents, especially his mother. For the painfully honest young Gandhi, this dubious experiment was simply not worth pursuing.

At the age of thirteen Mohandas married Kasturbai, the daughter of a cloth merchant who was the same age as him. An older Gandhi would see no moral argument in support of child marriage but at thirteen, it meant nothing more to him than "the prospect of good clothes, drum-beating, rich dinners and a strange little girl to play with."

Although shy, Mohandas quickly learned the role of a passionate, jealous and exacting husband. Both children had a will and temper of their own but Kasturbai, quiet and strong-willed, was not one to give in meekly to her young husband's autocratic ways. In Gandhi's youthful mind he was Kasturbai's teacher. Many years later, a suitably chastened Gandhi would recall:

I learnt the lesson of non-violence from my wife when I tried to bend her to my will. Her determined resistance to my will on the one hand, and her quiet submission on the other, ultimately made me ashamed of myself and cured me of my stupidity in thinking that I was born to rule over her. In the end she became my teacher in non-violence.

When Gandhi was still in school, his father fell ill. As the young Mohandas sat by his ailing father, devotedly nursing him, he was witness to many conversations between his father and his friends of different faiths. During this time, his interest in various religions grew. A conviction that took root in him during this time was that truth was the substance of all morality. A Gujarati verse which talked about "return good for evil" became his guiding principle.

Karamchand Gandhi succumbed to his illness and died when Mohandas was sixteen years old. At that time, Mohandas, preoccupied with the desirable company of his young wife, was not present at his father's side.

The guilt of this haunted Gandhi throughout his life.

If animal passion had not blinded me, I should have been spared the torture of separation from my father during his last moments. I should have been massaging him and he would have died in my arms. The shame of my carnal desire at the critical hour of my father's death is a blot I have never been able to efface or forget.

Paani aapne paay, bhalun bhojan tho deeje
Aavi namaave sheesh, dandavat kode keeje

Aapan ghaase dhaam, kaam mahoronun kariye
Aap ugare praan, te thanaa dukhma mariye

Gun kede tho gun dash gano man vaacha karame kari
Avgun kede jo gun kare, te jagma jeetyo sahi
Gujarati Bhajan – Traditional

For a bowl of water, give a goodly meal
For a kindly greeting, bow thou down with zeal
For a simple paisa, pay thou back with gold
If thy life be rescued, life do not withhold
Thus the words and actions of wise regard
Every little service tenfold they reward
But the truly noble know all men as one
And return gladness good for evil done

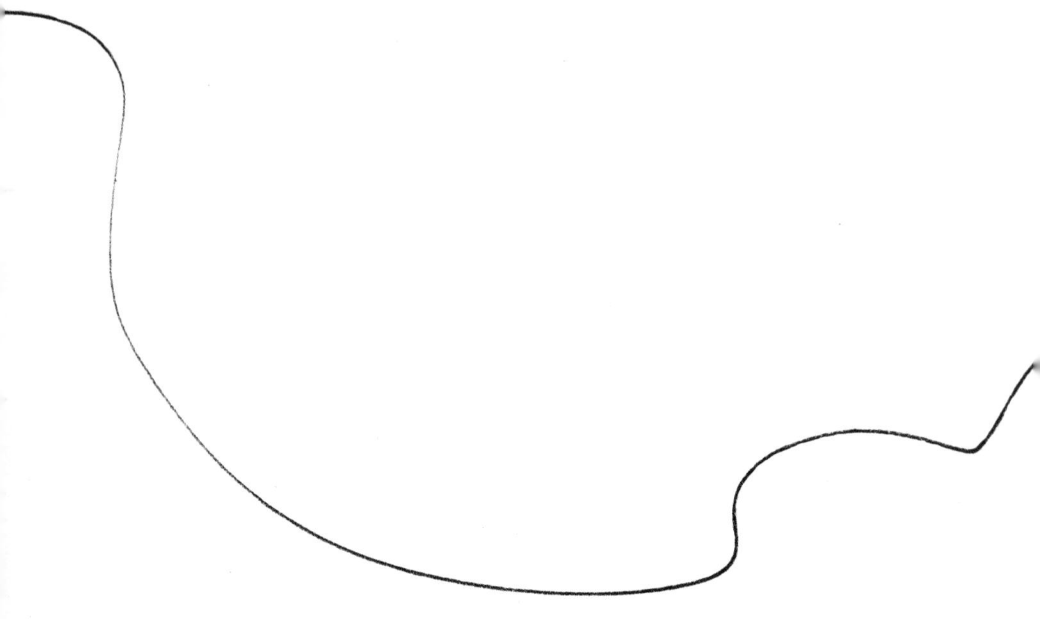

2

Gandhi's attempt at college was a disaster. Completely at sea, he failed in every class. After 5 months of consistent failure, he withdrew from college and returned home. He did not have the slightest idea of what to do. When a friend of the family suggested that he be sent to England for three years to study and become a barrister, Gandhi jumped at it.

On September 1888, just a month before his nineteenth birthday, with a solemn promise to his mother that he would not touch wine, women or meat, Gandhi boarded the S.S. Clyde from Bombay and set sail for England.

Gandhi's first few months in England were a nightmare.

Everything was strange – the people, their ways, and even their dwellings. I was a complete novice in the matter of English etiquette and continually had to be on guard. There was the additional inconvenience of the vegetarian vow. Even the dishes I could eat were tasteless and insipid. England I could not bear, but to return to India was not to be thought of. Now that I had come, I must finish the three years, said my inner voice.

Following a friend's advice he found a room with an English family. He even decided to cultivate a few habits of a pucca English gentleman in the hope of blending in.

The clothes that I was wearing were, I thought, unsuitable for English society. I got new ones at the Army and Navy stores. I also went for a chimney-pot hat, an evening suit, and got my brother to send me a double watch chain of gold. It was not correct to wear a ready-made tie, so I learnt the art of tying one.

As if all this was not enough to make me look the thing, I directed my attention to other details that were supposed to go towards the making of an English gentleman. I was told it was necessary for me to take lessons in dancing, French and elocution. I decided to take dancing lessons. But it was beyond me to achieve anything like rhythmic motion. I could not follow the piano and therefore found it impossible to keep time.

What then was I to do? Like the proverbial recluse who kept a cat to keep off the rats, and then a cow to feed that cat, and then a man to keep the cow, I thought I should learn to play the violin in order to cultivate an ear for Western music. So I bought a violin and got myself a teacher. I sought a third teacher to give me lessons in elocution. He recommended Bell's Standard Elocutionist, a text-book, but Mr. Bell rang the bell of alarm in my ear. I awoke.

I had not to spend a lifetime in England, I said to myself. What then was the use of learning elocution? How could dancing make a gentleman of me? I was a student here and ought to go on with my studies. If my character made a gentleman of me, so much the better. Otherwise I should forego the ambition.

Gandhi then began to experiment with a simpler way of life. He gave up all lessons in social etiquette, took a smaller room, cooked his own food, experimenting all the while with various diets, and walked to save on fares.

His long walks kept him alert and strong even in the harsh London winter, and formed a habit which he kept up throughout his life.

What began as an experiment to simplify his life, Gandhi would many years later evolve into the concept of voluntary poverty.

When I found myself drawn into the political coil, I asked myself what was necessary for me, in order to remain untouched by immorality, by untruth. I came to the conclusion that if I had to serve the people in whose midst my life was cast and of whose difficulties I was a witness from day to day, I must discard all wealth, all possession.

I must confess to you that the progress at first was slow. But as the days went by, I saw that I had to throw overboard many other things which I used to consider as mine, and a time came when it became a positive joy to give up those things. A great burden fell off my shoulders, and I felt that I could walk with ease and do my work also in the service of my fellow men with great comfort and still greater joy.

Gandhi's time in England was sober and disciplined, but lonely. He missed home and longed to be back in India. On June 10th, 1891, he passed his bar exam and the very next day he sailed for home.

The practice of law is not for the nervous and inarticulate, as Gandhi found to his dismay first in Bombay and then in Rajkot. Not only did he not know how to apply legal principles to particular situations, his English education left him without the slightest knowledge of Indian law. Bitter and bewildered, and out of tune with the atmosphere of petty intrigue that was rampant in Rajkot, he longed to escape from India.

At this point Gandhi's life took on one of those fateful turns.

A firm from Porbandar offered him a year's contract with its office in South Africa. Gandhi grabbed the opportunity. In April 1893, not yet twenty-four years old, Gandhi set sail to try his luck. In South Africa, this shy, timid and inexperienced youth would find more than luck. Here Gandhi would find himself, his philosophy and his following.

Nirbal ke bal Raam, nirbal ke bal Raam
Pichli saakh bharun santhan ki, aade sanwaare kaam

Jab lag gaj bal apno baratyo nek saro nahin kaam
Nirbal hai bal Raam pukaryo aaye aadhe naam
Sur kishor krupase sab bal, haare ko hari naam

Bhajan – Saint Surdas

Lord Rama is the might of the weak
I know of those saintly people who were helped by him
in their adversity

Even an elephant who relied upon his own strength,
remained helpless
But in his helplessness when he invoked the assistance of
Rama, he responded when hardly his name was half pronounced

Surdas says that when the weak invoke the name of God,
His grace descends upon them

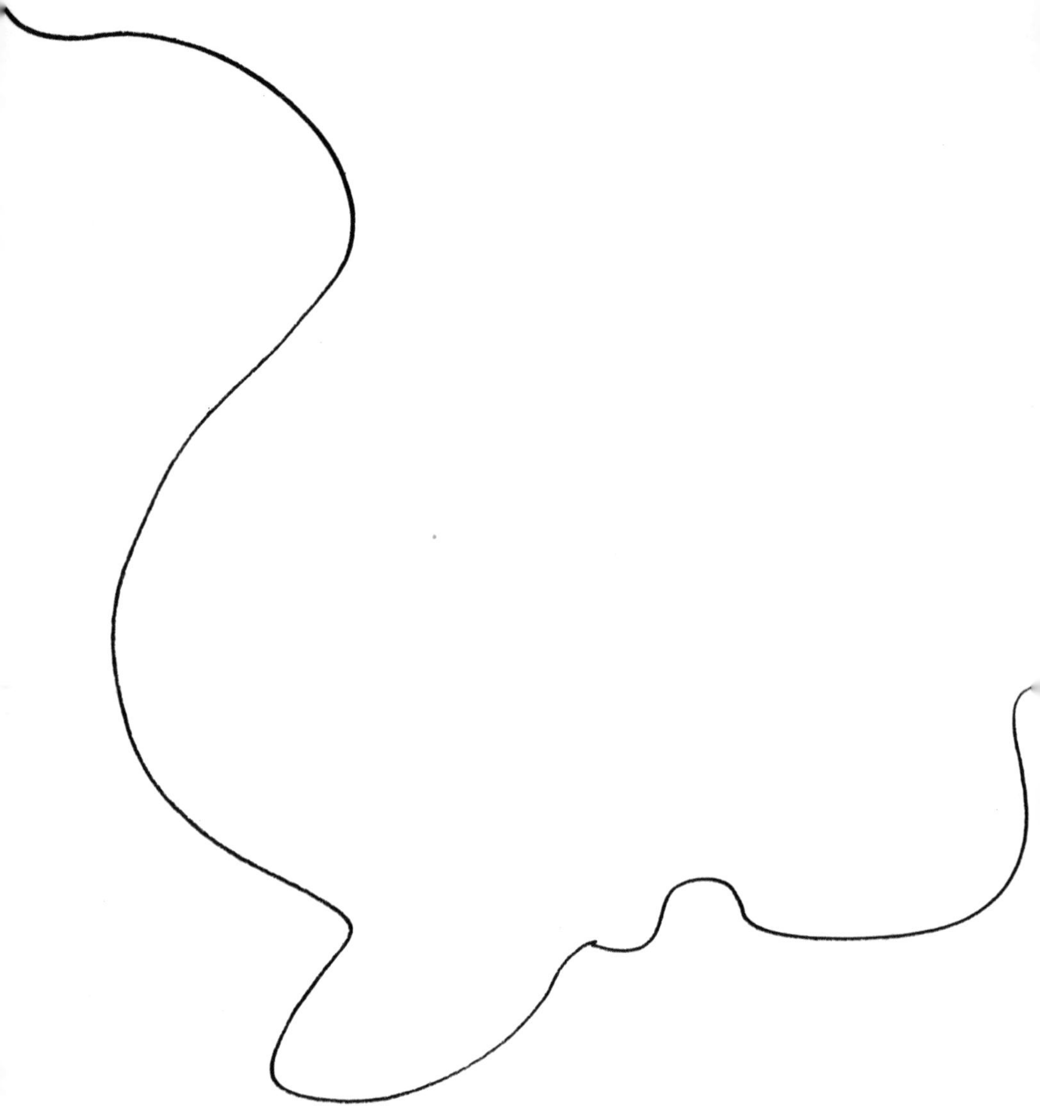

3

South Africa at that time was divided into four areas. Natal and the Cape Colony were British possessions, and the Orange Free State and the Transvaal were held by the Dutch.

At the end of the nineteenth century there were approximately sixty-five thousand Indians in South Africa. The first had come as serfs, bound to five years of plantation labour. There were also thousands of free Indians of all classes. Some of them had become wealthy and powerful. This outraged and frightened the Europeans, who would not consider coloured men equals, and who contemptuously referred to the Indians as "coolies".

Abdulla Sheth, a partner in the firm I was representing, was at Durban to receive me. As the ship arrived at the quay and I watched the people coming on board to meet their friends, I observed that Indians were not held in much respect. I could not fail to note a sort of snobbishness about the manner in which those who knew Abdulla Sheth behaved towards him.

On the second or third day of my arrival, Abdulla Sheth took me to see the Durban court. The magistrate kept staring at me and finally asked me to take off my turban. I refused and left the court. I wrote to the press about the incident and defended the wearing of my turban. The question was very much discussed in the papers, which described me as an "unwelcome visitor". The whole affair gave me an unexpected advertisement in South Africa within a few days of my arrival there. My turban stayed with me practically until the end of my stay.

Whilst I was widening the circle of my acquaintance, the firm received a letter from their lawyers saying preparations should be made for the case. Abdulla Sheth asked me if I could go to Pretoria as his representative. I agreed and a few days later, left Durban for Pretoria.

A first class seat was booked for me. The train reached Maritzburg, the capital of Natal, at about 9 p.m. A passenger came and looked me up and down. Out he went and came in again with one or two officials.

One of them came to me and said, "Come along, you must go to the van compartment."

"But I have a first class ticket," said I.

"That doesn't matter, I tell you. You must go to the van compartment."

When I refused again, the man threatened to call a police constable.

The constable came. He took me by the hand and pushed me out. My luggage was also taken out. I refused to go to the van compartment and the train steamed away. I went and sat in the waiting room.

It was winter. Maritzburg being at a high altitude, the cold was extremely bitter. My overcoat was in my luggage, but I did not dare ask for it. There was no light in the room. I sat and shivered.

I began to think of what I should do. Should I fight for my rights, should I go back to India, or should I go on to Pretoria, and return to India after finishing the case? It would be cowardice to run back to India without fulfilling my obligations. The hardship to which I was subjected was only a symptom of the deep disease of colour prejudice. I should try, if possible, to root out the disease and suffer hardships in the process. So I decided to take the next available train to Pretoria.

At every stage on his way to Pretoria, Gandhi experienced the prevailing racial prejudice. The journey was to change Gandhi's life. In Pretoria, Indians could not own property. They could not vote. They were not allowed to walk on public footpaths. They could not even go outdoors after 9 p.m. without a permit.

Gandhi called a meeting of the Indians in Pretoria. He made his first public speech that night; indignation had finally freed his shy tongue.

My speech at this meeting was the first public speech in my life. I went fairly prepared with my subject, which was about observing truthfulness in business. I had always heard the merchants say that truth was not possible in business. I did not think so then, nor do I now. I awakened the merchants to a sense of their duty, which was twofold. Their responsibility to be truthful was all the greater in a foreign land, because the conduct of a few Indians was a measure of that of the millions of their fellow-countrymen.

I had found our people's habits to be unsanitary, and drew their attention to it. I laid stress on the necessity of forgetting all distinctions such as Hindus, Mussalmans, Parsis, Christians, Gujaratis, Madrasis, Punjabis, Sindhis and so on. I saw that very few amongst my audience knew English. I advised those who had the leisure to learn the language.

In the meantime, Gandhi had to attend to the case of Sheth Abdulla. Gandhi saw that the cost of litigation was very high, and if the case went on, both the parties would be ruined. He persuaded them to agree to a compromise and the case was finally settled out of court.

In turning his back on personal profit, Gandhi found that he had won the trust and love of the Indians in South Africa. More and more people began to entrust their legal work to him. He strove for solutions that would benefit everyone. He trusted the essential goodness of people and the ultimate triumph of good over evil.

Following a case involving a Tamil labourer, he came to be known as the friend and champion of the bonded labourers.

A Tamil man in tattered clothes, headgear in hand, two front teeth broken and his mouth bleeding, stood before me, trembling and weeping. He had been heavily belaboured by his master. His name was Balasundaram. He was serving his indenture under a well-known European resident of Durban. I secured a certificate from a doctor and took the injured man to the magistrate. The magistrate was indignant and issued summons against the employer.

I had no desire to get the employer punished. I simply wanted Balasundaram to be released from him. I called on the latter and convinced him that I would not proceed against him, and requested him to transfer the indenture to someone else. He readily agreed to this, and the indenture was transferred.

Balasundaram's case reached the ears of every indentured labourer and I came to be regarded as their friend. There was nothing extraordinary in the case itself, but the fact that there was someone in Natal to espouse their cause and publicly work for them, inspired the indentured labourers with hope.

I have said that Balasundaram entered my office, headgear in hand. A practice had been forced upon every indentured labourer and every Indian stranger to take off his headgear when visiting a European. Balasundaram thought that he should follow this practice even with me. I felt mortified and asked him to tie up his scarf. He did so, not without hesitation, but I could perceive the pleasure on his face.

It has always been a mystery to me how men can feel themselves honoured by the humiliation of their fellow-beings.

The idea of selfless service had taken hold of Gandhi and he underwent a transformation in every aspect of his life. Everywhere he began to see the possibility to choose between living for himself and living for others.

Vaishnav jan tho thene kahiye
Je peedh parayi jaane re
Par dukhe upkaar kare thoye
Man abhimaan na aane re

Van lobhi ne kapat rahit che
Kaam krodh nivarya re
Bhane Narsayyo thenun darshan kartha
Kul ekother tarya re
Bhajan – Saint Narsinh Mehta

A godlike man is one
Who feels another's pain
Who shares another's sorrow
And pride does disdain

One who is not greedy and deceitful
And has conquered lust and anger
Through such a man, Saint Narsaiyon has a godly vision
Generations to come, of such a man will attain salvation

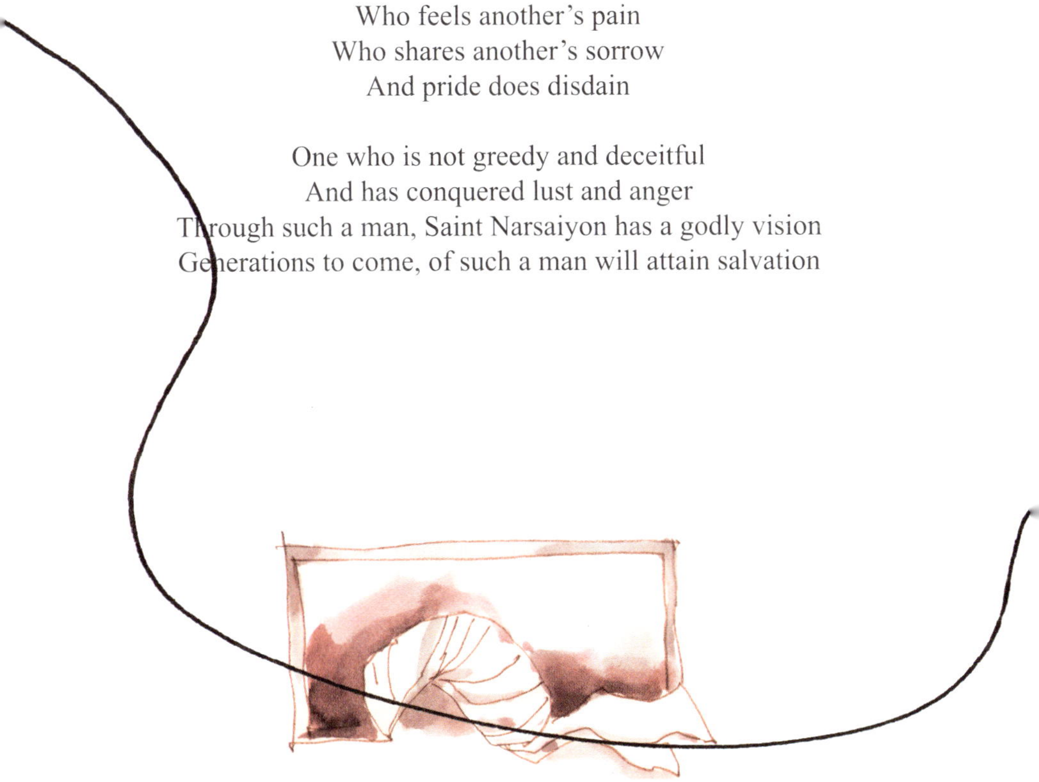

4

With Sheth Abdulla's case resolved, Gandhi's job in South Africa was done. He decided to return to India. But this was not to be. At a farewell party in his honour he noticed a newspaper item about a bill which would deprive Natal Indians of the right to vote. The Indians pleaded with Gandhi to stay.

Gandhi stayed on and the farewell party transformed into a planning session for a crusade for civil rights.

The crusade would last twenty years and evolve and test the essential weapons of every non-violent freedom movement of the twentieth century.

At the end of three years, having formed the Natal Indian Congress to direct the agitation of Indian rights, Gandhi decided to go home for six months and return with Kasturbai and their two sons. The year was 1896.

Back in India, the independence movement was gaining strength, and during this visit, Gandhi made the acquaintance of veteran leaders like Badruddin Tyabji, Pherozeshah Mehta, Surendranath Banerjee and the great savant and patriot, Bal Gangadhar Tilak. He also met the wise and noble-hearted Gopal Krishna Gokhale and was greatly drawn to him. Of all the leaders he met, Gokhale had the greatest influence on Gandhi.

While in India, Gandhi traveled extensively, drumming up sympathy for the plight of the South African Indians. Outraged, he gave newspaper interviews, made speeches, and wrote a pamphlet which was widely distributed.

When Gandhi returned to Durban with his family, his ship was put into quarantine. The European community had been led to believe that Gandhi had condemned them in his pamphlet. They also thought he was trying to swamp Natal with Indians. Wild with anger, they threatened to drown all the passengers. Gandhi was once again an unwelcome visitor.

As soon as we landed, some youngsters recognized me and shouted, "Gandhi, Gandhi." About half a dozen men rushed to the spot. As we went ahead, the crowd continued to swell, until it became impossible to go further. They first caught hold of my companion, Mr. Laughton and then separated us. Then they pelted me with stones, brickbats and rotten eggs. Someone snatched away my turban, while others began to beat me and kick me. The wife of the police superintendent, Mrs. Alexander, who knew me, happened to be passing by. She came up, opened her umbrella and stood between the crowd and me. This checked the fury of the mob, as it was difficult for them to deliver blows on me without harming Mrs. Alexander.

Meanwhile an Indian youth who had witnessed the incident had run to the police station. The Police Superintendent, Mr. Alexander, sent a few men to take me safely to my destination. I had bruises all over.

There was quiet inside, but outside the whites surrounded the house. Night was coming on, and the yelling crowd was shouting, "We must have Gandhi." The Police Superintendent said that I should escape from the house in disguise.

So I put on an Indian constable's uniform and wore on my head a Madrasi scarf, wrapped round a plate to serve as a helmet. Two detectives in disguise accompanied me. We reached a neighbouring shop through a by-lane and escaped to a carriage that had been kept for me at the end of the street.

Mr. Escombe, a member of the Cabinet, sent for me, expressed his regret for the injuries I had sustained, and offered to arrest and prosecute my assailants.

But I told Mr. Escombe that I did not intend to prosecute anyone.

This magnanimous gesture astounded the Europeans and when Gandhi explained the true contents of the Green Pamphlet, the European community was placated. His reputation grew and the prestige of the Indian community rose.

It was 1901 when Gandhi once again returned to India. He always travelled third class in crowded, dirty compartments to experience the difficulties of the poor. When someone asked him why he only travelled third class, he answered simply, "Because there is no fourth!" It was during one such travel that a cablegram from the Indian community in Natal recalled him. Leaving his family in India, he sailed yet again for South Africa.

The work confronting Gandhi when he returned to South Africa would keep him there for the next thirteen years.

It was a turbulent time for him, both politically and personally.

On the political front, there were many battles to be fought. The South African government was adopting stringent anti-Indian policies, and depriving Indians of even elementary civic rights. Gandhi launched into war. But his was not a battle of weaponry or vitriolic words. Non-violence was his creed. He repeatedly defied the dictates of the government, and encouraged his co-workers to do the same. Gandhi became their unquestioned leader.

While he worked, his political aims continued to fuse with his spiritual and emotional life. The Bhagavad Gita became his guide, his spiritual reference book and he embraced its teaching that truth could be gained only through renunciation of all possessions and all pleasures.

In 1906, not quite thirty-seven years old, he took a vow of Brahmacharya or celibacy which he never broke, and the bride of his childhood, Kasturbai, became not so much a wife as the most devoted of his followers.

Brahmacharya means control of the senses in thought, word and deed. There is no limit to the possibilities of renunciation, even as there is none to those of Brahmacharya. The knowledge that a perfect observance of Brahmacharya means realization of Brahman or Truth, I did not owe to the study of the Shastras. It slowly grew upon me with experience. Every day of the vow has taken me nearer the knowledge that in Brahmacharya lies the protection of the body, the mind and the soul. For Brahmacharya was now no process of hard penance, it was a matter of great joy. Every day revealed a fresh beauty in it.

But if it was a matter of ever increasing joy, let no one believe that it was an easy thing for me. Even when I am past fifty-six years, I realize how hard a thing it is. Every day, I realize more and more that it is like walking on the sword's edge, and I see every moment the necessity of eternal vigilance.

It was also during this period, that the principle of Satyagraha came into being. Gandhi knew from his own deep and vast experience that no brute force could quell the spirit of man ready to defy and willing to suffer. He believed that the Indians' cause could be won by a method that embraced the principles of truth or Satya, and non-violence or Ahimsa.

At first he called this method 'passive resistance'. But the struggle of the Indians in South Africa was unique and unprecedented; it needed a new word. His cousin, Maganlal Gandhi, suggested the word "Sadagraha", meaning firmness in a good cause. Gandhi modified it to Satyagraha and thus developed his most original and powerful weapon in political action.

Satyagraha is the vindication of truth not by infliction of suffering on the opponent but on oneself. The fight of Satyagraha is for the strong in spirit, not the doubter or the timid. Satyagraha teaches us the art of living as well as dying.

By the end of the Satyagraha struggle, Gandhi had spent twenty years in South Africa. The world had seen the dawning of a new kind of warrior and a new art of warfare. In South Africa it had eliminated the worst of the anti-Indian abuses. In India it was to crumble an empire and create a new nation.

Deva dwija guru praagya poojanam shoucha maarjavam
Brahmacharyam ahimsaacha shaariram tapa uchyate
Shloka – Bhagavad Gita

Worship of the Lord, the brahmanas, the guru, and elders,
in cleanliness, simplicity, celibacy and nonviolence:
these constitute the austerity of the body

Ahimsaa satyam akrodha
Tyaagah shaantir apaya shunam
Dayaa bhooteshya loluptvam
Maardhavam sreera chaapalam

Tejakshamaa driti shoucham
Adroho naati maanita
Bhavanti sampadam daiveem
Abhijaatasya bhaarataa
Shloka – Bhagavad Gita

Non-violence, truthfulness, freedom from anger
Renunciation, tranquility, aversion to slander
Compassion for all living beings, freedom from sensuality
Gentleness, modesty, steadfastness

Vigour, forgiveness, fortitude, purity
Harmlessness, freedom from vanity
These transcendental qualities, O son of Bharata
Belong to godly men endowed with divine nature

5

When Gandhi returned to India the drive for independence had an end but no means. As early as 1906, India's only political voice, the Indian National Congress demanded self-government but the words did not carry all the way back to London.

Gandhi did not immediately involve himself in the Indian independence movement. Although a few people had heard of the remarkable impact he had made in South Africa, he was not very well known in India. Nor did Gandhi know his India well. He therefore readily promised Gokhale, his political guru, that he would spend his first year in India studying the country.

Village upliftment was Gandhi's first focus. Over 80% of India lived in her villages, and they were poor, diseased, illiterate and discouraged. Gandhi was convinced that once the peasants acquired individual dignity, nobody could hold them in bondage.

I have believed and repeated times without number that India is to be found not in its cities but in its 700,000 villages. It is the villages we have to turn to. We have to disabuse them of their prejudices, their superstitions, their narrow outlook, and we can do so in no other manner than staying amongst them, sharing their joys and sorrows, and spreading education and intelligent information among them. If the village perishes, India will perish too. The revival of the village is possible only when it is no longer exploited.

Meanwhile, now that he and his large entourage were back in India, Gandhi needed a home.

I wanted to have an Ashram where I could settle down with my family, preferably somewhere in Gujarat. The Satyagraha Ashram was founded on the 25th of May, 1915 at Kochrab in Ahmedabad.

We were in all about twenty-five men and women. We had our meals in a common kitchen and strove to live as one family.

The Ashram had been in existence only a few months when we were put to a test such as I scarcely expected. I received a letter to this effect: "A humble and honest untouchable family is desirous of joining your Ashram. Will you accept them?"

I wrote back expressing our willingness to accept the family, provided all the members were ready to abide by the rules of the Ashram. They agreed and were accepted.

But their admission created a stir amongst the friends who had been helping in the Ashram. In addition, all monetary help was stopped. With this came rumours of proposed social boycott. We were prepared for all this. I had told my companions that, if we were boycotted and denied the usual facilities, we would not leave Ahmedabad. We would rather go and stay in the 'untouchables' quarter and live on whatever we could get by manual labour.

Sure enough, Maganlal Gandhi one day gave me the notice that we were out of funds and did not have any provisions for the next month. I declared that we could go to the 'untouchables' quarter.

One morning shortly after this, one of the children came and said a Sheth who was waiting in a car outside wanted to see me. I went out to him. He placed in my hands 13,000 rupees and drove away.

I had never expected this help, and what a novel way of rendering it. The gentleman had never before visited the Ashram. No visit, no enquiries, he simply rendered help and went away. This was a unique experience for me.

The admission of the 'untouchable' family proved a valuable lesson to the Ashram. Right from the beginning we proclaimed to the world that the Ashram would not sanction untouchability. The fact that it was mostly the orthodox Hindus who met the growing expenses of the Ashram was a clear indication that untouchability was shaken to its foundation.

Gandhi travelled around India, getting to know the country. Even though he was not yet a national figure, people were beginning to hear about this frail man who was a champion of the poor and the dispossessed. They were beginning to call him the Mahatma – or the "Great Soul", a title conferred upon him by his friend, the poet, Rabindranath Tagore. However, no matter where he travelled, Gandhi always returned to the Sabarmati Ashram. This was the third of his ashrams after the Phoenix settlement and the Tolstoy farm in South Africa.

It was Champaran, a small village in Bihar that thrust Gandhi on the national stage.

The Champaran peasant was bound by law to plant three out of every twenty parts of his land with the commercial crop, indigo, for his British landlord. Gandhi went to Champaran to investigate their complaints and was advised by the British commissioner to leave. When he ignored the warning, he received an official notice ordering him out of the district. He refused to go and was summoned to court.

On the day of the trial, masses of peasants appeared in town in a spontaneous demonstration of solidarity. The officials were bewildered and a little frightened. They were even more perplexed when Gandhi pleaded guilty. Judgement was postponed and in a few days, the case was withdrawn. It was the first victory of civil disobedience in India.

Defeated by the defiance of the peasants, the government finally appointed a commission of inquiry, which ruled in favour of the peasants.

Soon after this, Gandhi was called to Ahmedabad to help the mill-workers in their struggle for better wages and conditions. Gandhi advised the labourers to go on strike. However, he laid down some ground rules: never resort to violence; never depend on charity; earn bread through some kind of labour; and remain firm, no matter how long the strike continues. The labourers gave their word. But after a couple of weeks, their resolve began to weaken.

The mill-hands' attendance at their daily meetings began to dwindle, and despondency and despair were writ large on the faces of those who did attend. I felt deeply troubled and set to think furiously as to what I should do. The mill hands had taken the pledge at my suggestion and the very idea that they might now go back upon it, to me, was inconceivable. Was it pride or was it my love for the labourers and my passionate regard for truth that was at the back of this feeling – who can say?

One morning, while I was still groping and unable to see my way clearly, the light came to me. Unbidden the words came to my lips, "Unless the strikers rally," I declared to the meeting, "and continue the strike till a settlement is reached, or till they leave the mills altogether, I will not touch any food."

The labourers were thunderstruck. They broke out, "Not you, but we shall fast. It would be monstrous if you were to fast. Please forgive us our lapse; we will now remain faithful to our pledge to the end."

My fast was not free from a grave defect. I enjoyed close and cordial relations with the mill owners and my fast could not but affect their decision. As a Satyagrahi, I knew that I might not fast against them, but ought to leave them free to be influenced by the mill-hands' strike alone. Yet, in spite of my knowledge that my fast was bound to put pressure on the mill-owners, as in fact it did, I felt I could not help it.

However, the net result was that an atmosphere of goodwill was created. The hearts of the mill-owners were touched. The strike was called off after I had fasted only for three days. A settlement was reached after twenty-one days of strike.

This was Gandhi's first public fast. Over the years the weapon of fasting became so powerful, so simple, so effective and so dramatic that he came to regard it as an essential part of his armoury.

When I survey the wondrous cross
On which the Prince of Glory died
My richest gain I count but loss
And pour contempt on all my pride

Were the whole realm of nature mine
That were a present far too small
Love so amazing, so divine
Demands my soul, my life, my all
Hymn – Isaac Watts

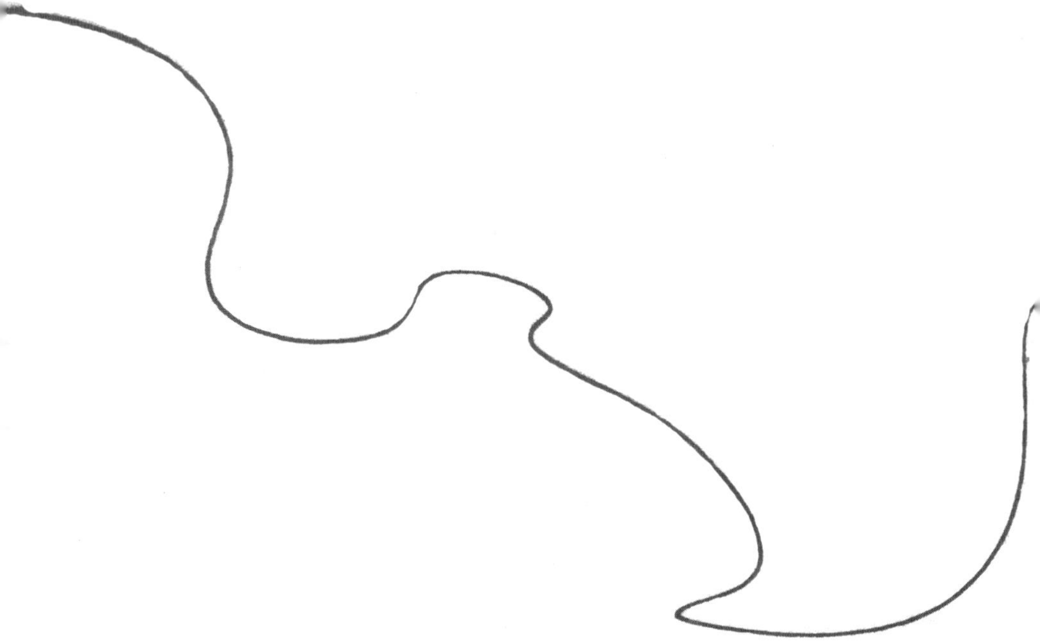

6

It was 1919 and World War I had ended. The Indians had expected to have their civil liberties restored at the end of the war, but instead, a British commission headed by Sir Sidney Rowlatt went to India to study the situation.

It was the Rowlatt Act with its denial of civil liberties which finally brought Gandhi into active Indian politics. The Act authorized arrest and detention, without trial, of anyone suspected of anti-government activities. Gandhi wondered what could be done. The solution came to him in a dream. He declared that the country would observe a general hartal, or stoppage of work, for one day.

April 6th, 1919 saw the whole country from one end to the other, towns as well as villages, come to a stunning standstill. But Gandhi had unleashed forces he could not contain. He was deeply saddened and horrified when the Indians followed the hartal with violence, looting, and murder.

On the night of the 7th I started for Delhi and Amritsar. But I was prohibited from entering the boundary of the Punjab. At Palwal railway station, I was taken out of the train and put under police custody. The next morning, I was put in a goods train that was going towards Bombay. I was released at Bombay.

There was a great disturbance in the city owing to my arrest. A huge crowd had gathered. On seeing me, the people went mad with joy. A procession was immediately formed. Suddenly, mounted police arrived there to prevent the crowd from proceeding further. The officer-in-charge gave the order to disperse the crowd, and at once the mounted police charged upon the crowd on their horses, brandishing their lances as they went. The ranks of the people were soon broken, and they were thrown into utter confusion. They began to run. Some got trampled under foot; others were badly hurt and crushed. The whole thing presented a most dreadful spectacle.

News came of disturbances in Ahmedabad as well. Someone had spread a rumour that the mill-hands had gone berserk and committed acts of violence. Martial law had been declared. I proceeded to Ahmedabad.

I asked the Commissioner for permission to hold a public meeting on the grounds of the Sabarmati Ashram. Addressing the meeting, I tried to bring home to the people the sense of their wrongdoing. It was unbearable for me to find that the labourers, whom I had served, and from whom I had expected better things, had taken part in the riots. I shared their guilt. Just as I suggested to the people to confess their guilt, I suggested to the government to condone their crimes. Neither accepted my suggestion.

I made up my mind to suspend Satyagraha so long as people had not learnt the lesson of peace. If those amongst whom I worked, and whom I expected to be prepared for non-violence and self-suffering, could not be so, Satyagraha was certainly impossible. I realized that I had committed a Himalayan blunder. I confessed this at a public meeting in Nadiad. My confession brought upon me a large amount of ridicule. But I have never regretted making it. For I have always held that when one sees one's own mistakes with a convex lens, and does just the reverse in the case of others, that one is then able to arrive at a just relative estimate of the two.

Let me explain what the Himalayan blunder was. Before one can be fit for the practice of civil disobedience, one must have rendered a willing and respectful obedience to the state laws. A Satyagrahi obeys the laws of society intelligently and of his own free will. It is only when a person has thus obeyed the laws of society scrupulously that he is in a position to judge as to which rules are good and just, and which unjust and iniquitous. Only then does the right accrue to him of the civil disobedience of certain laws in well-defined circumstances. My error lay in my failure to observe this necessary limitation. I had called on the people to launch civil disobedience before they had thus qualified themselves for it.

I reached Bombay and raised a corps of Satyagrahi volunteers, and with their help commenced the work of educating the people with regard to the meaning and inner significance of Satyagraha.

Gandhi's critics often complained that he would withdraw from a political struggle just when it was on the verge of success. But for Gandhi, success had to be moral and spiritual; not merely political. For him, the end could never justify the means.

Meanwhile, Punjab was boiling with anti-British violence and the Punjab government declared martial law. On April 13, 1919, at Jallianwala Bagh in Amritsar, hundreds of men, women and children were cold-bloodedly massacred by soldiers, who opened fire on them as they tried to escape from the enclosed grounds.

After repeated requests to the government, Gandhi was finally permitted to go to Punjab in October. Gandhi assisted in an independent Indian inquiry into the atrocity. He then proceeded to Delhi for the Khilafat Conference. It was at this conference that the idea of non-cooperation was born.

Among the numerous resolutions that were passed at this conference, one called upon both, Hindus and Mussalmans, to take the Swadeshi vow, and as a natural corollary to it, boycott foreign goods. I felt that something new, over and above boycott of foreign cloth would be necessary. I could not hit upon a suitable Urdu or Hindi word for the new idea, and that put me out somewhat. At last I hit upon the word 'non-cooperation', an expression that I used for the first time at this meeting. It was vain to talk of resistance to the Government with which one was cooperating in more ways than one. The only true resistance to the Government, it therefore seemed to me, was to cease to cooperate with it.

Ahimsa, Satyagraha and now Non-Cooperation. Gandhi's arsenal of non-violent weapons was now complete.

Satya ahimsa chori na karvi
Van jo tu nav sangharvu
Brahmacharya ne jaat mehnat
Koi adhe na abhdaavu

Abhay swadeshi swaarth tyaag ne
Sarv dharma sarkhaa ganvaa
Aa agiyaar mahaavrat samjhi
Dhradpane nitya aacharva

Gujarati Bhajan

Truth, non-violence, non-stealing
Non-possession
Celibacy, physical labour,
And removal of untouchability

Fearlessness, national spirit, selflessness
And equal respect towards all religions
These eleven vows
Follow them strictly everyday

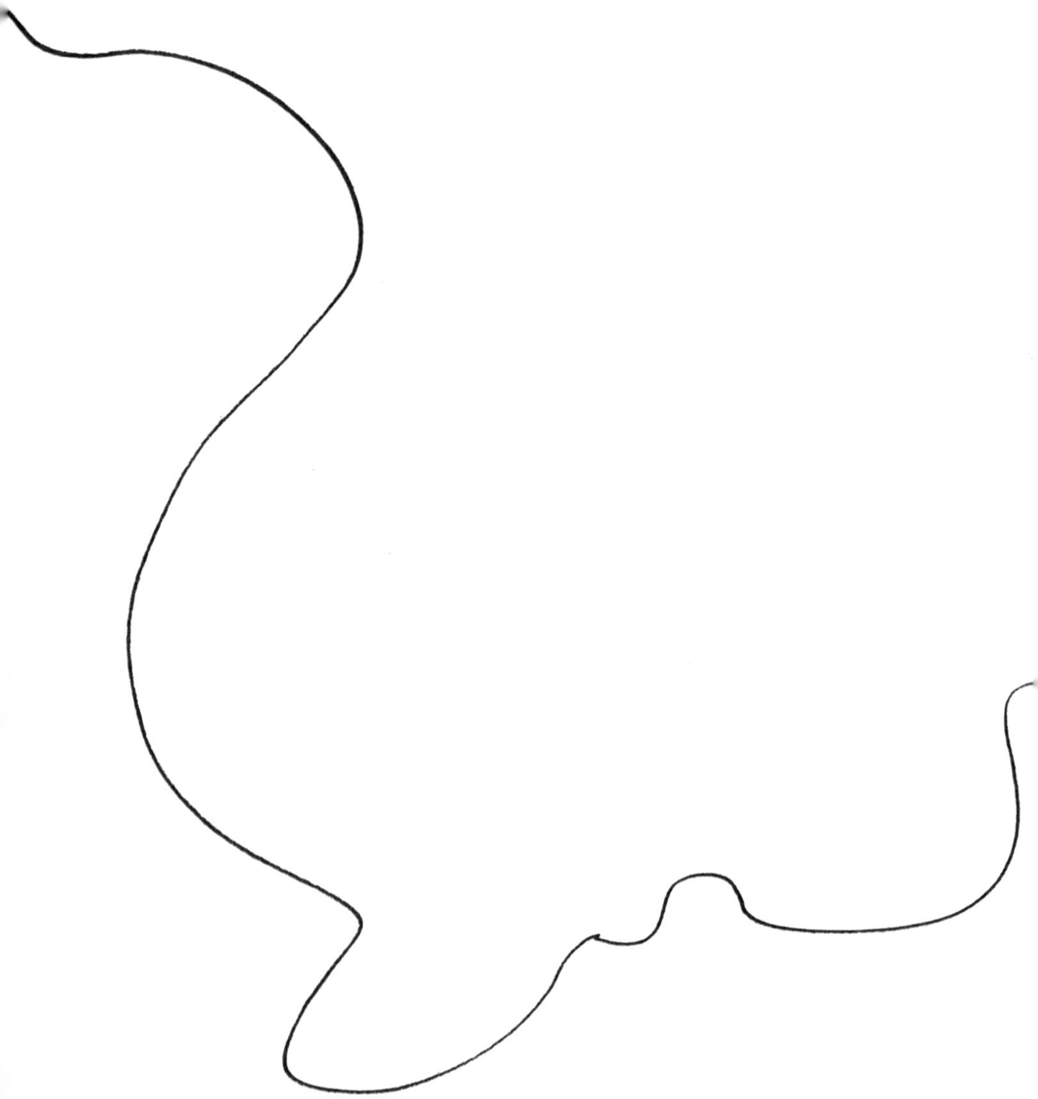

7

Even as Gandhi was getting more and more involved in Indian politics, he was also pursuing another idea, the revival of the charkha or the spinning wheel. Gandhi wanted to promote the use of khadi or homespun cotton. But for that, it was necessary to master the spinning wheel.

In my book Hind Swaraj, I have described the spinning wheel as the panacea for the growing pauperism of India. My premise was that anything that helped India get rid of the grinding poverty of her masses would in the same process also establish Swaraj or Home Rule.

When the Satyagraha Ashram was founded at Sabarmati, we introduced a few handlooms there.

The object that we in the Ashram set before ourselves was to be able to clothe ourselves entirely in cloth manufactured by our own hands. We therefore forthwith gave up the use of mill-made cloth and all the members of the Ashram resolved to wear hand-woven cloth, made from Indian yarn only. We had to depend on the mills for the yarn, and we became impatient to be able to spin our own yarn.

But we could get neither a spinning wheel nor a spinner to teach us how to spin. I plied every chance visitor to the Ashram, who was likely to possess some information about hand spinning, with questions about the art.

In the year 1917, at the Broach Educational Conference, I discovered that remarkable lady, Gangabehn Majumdar. To her I poured out my grief about the spinning wheel, and she lightened my burden by a promise to search for the spinning wheel till she found it.

At last, after no end of wandering in Gujarat, Gangabehn found the spinning wheel in Vijapur in the Baroda State. Quite a number of people there had spinning wheels in their homes, but had long since put them away as useless lumber. They were ready to resume spinning, if someone promised to buy the yarn spun by them. Gangabehn communicated the joyful news to me, and the spinning wheel gained a rapid footing in the Ashram.

The Swadeshi movement had begun. In time, there would be hundreds and thousands of spinning wheels across the nation. Gandhi exhorted people to learn how to spin and weave. Through spinning, Gandhi was convinced that the people of the 700,000 impoverished villages of India could regain self-employment, self-reliance and self-respect.

To Gandhi spinning was prayer. In the hum of the spinning wheel, he found solace. Khadi also came to represent simplicity and a spirit of nationalism.

In 1927, Gandhi wrote in Young India:

If we have the khadi spirit in us, we would surround ourselves with simplicity in every walk of life. The khadi spirit means unlimited patience. For those who know anything about the production of khadi, know how patiently the spinners and the weavers have to toil at their trade, and even so must we have patience while we are spinning 'the thread of swaraj'.

The 'khadi spirit' means a fellow feeling with every human being on earth. It means a complete renunciation of everything that is likely to harm our fellow creatures, and if we but cultivate that spirit amongst the millions of our countrymen, what a land this India of ours would be! And the more I move about the country and the more I see things for myself, the richer, the stronger is my faith growing in the capacity of the spinning wheel.

When the time came to design the flag of independent India, the spinning wheel came to occupy a central position.

When Gandhi was arrested in 1922 and sentenced to six years in prison, he took his spinning wheel to jail with him. He contentedly spun, read and worked on his autobiography.

The Story of My Experiments with Truth, ends in 1920.

From 1919 to his death in 1948, he occupied the centre stage of India's struggle for freedom and was the hero of the great historical drama that culminated in the independence of his country. Into the turbulent world of Indian politics, the Mahatma came as a maverick, wielding the unlikely weapons of Ahimsa and Satyagraha.

He died as he always lived, without wealth or property, and without title or office.

In the words of Albert Einstein, “Generations to come will scarcely believe that such a one as this, ever in flesh and blood, walked upon this earth.”

With an indomitable belief in “Satyameva Jayate” or “Truth will prevail”, Mohandas Karamchand Gandhi, the iconic small brown man in a loin cloth, defied and baffled the British government; led India to freedom and became Bapu, the Father of the Nation.

Raghupati Raghav Raaja Raam
Pateet paavan Seetaa Raam
Eshwar Allah tero naam
Sabko sanmathi de bhagwaan

Hindi Bhajan

Although we call you by different names, you are One
Give us the wisdom to understand this, O Lord

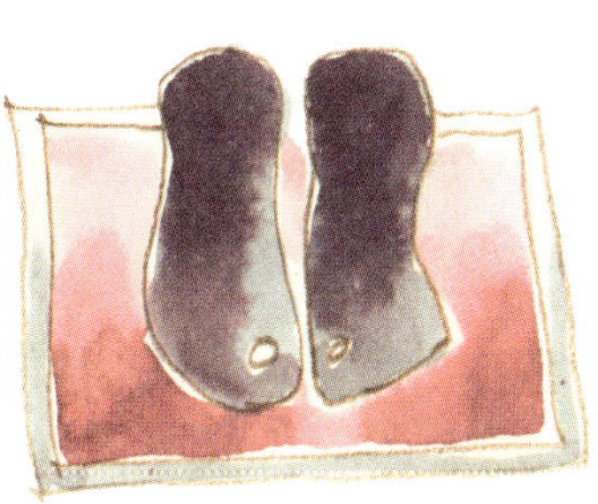

Farewell

The time has now come to bring these chapters to a close.

My life from this point onward has been so public that there is hardly anything about it that people do not know. In fact, my pen instinctively refuses to proceed further.

It is not without regret that I have to take leave of the reader.

I set a high value on my experiments. I do not know whether I have been able to do justice to them. I can only say that I have spared no pains to give a faithful narrative. To describe truth as it appeared to me has been my ceaseless effort. The exercise has given me great mental peace, because it has been my fond hope that it might bring faith in Truth and Ahimsa to all. In bidding farewell to the reader, I ask him to join me in prayer to the God of Truth that He may grant me the boon of Ahimsa in mind, word and deed.

Shaanti nilava vendum
Aatma shakti onga vendum, ulagile

Gandhi mahaatma kattalai adhuve
Karunai otrumai kadhiroli paravi

Tamil Kriti – Sadasiva Rao

May peace prevail in the world
May fortitude spring forth from every soul

Gandhi Mahatma asks thus
That we embrace all, in the light of compassion and oneness

Conclusion*

The story of Mahatma Gandhi's life after 1919 is inseparable from the story of India's fight for freedom.

By 1919, Gandhi had become the bulwark of the Congress. The Congress, until then, was largely controlled by a group of wealthy, anglicized members. At the Nagpur session in 1920, the Congress adopted a new constitution, drafted by Gandhi, which converted it into a democratic mass organization. At Congress sessions people wore khadi, and spoke Hindustani, rather than English. Along with the middle-class majority, there were now some delegates from among the poor.

After the Nagpur Congress, Gandhi carried his message of non-cooperation to the masses, who responded enthusiastically. Throughout the country people boycotted British cloth, education, jobs and taxes. Gandhi travelled all over India, in the heat and humidity, sleeping on trains and living on bread, fruit and milk. Everywhere he went, Indians came in hordes to see the Mahatma. And when he

* Not included in audio

asked them to discard their foreign clothing, they willingly threw their clothes onto a pile, and Gandhi set fire to them.

It was in 1921 that Gandhi discarded his cap, waistcoat and flowing dhoti and replaced them with a khadi loincloth. Khadi became a symbol of nationalism, and soon, no Indian leader would think of going into the rural areas clad in anything but the humble khadi.

By this time, most of his followers had taken to calling Gandhi, Bapu – or father. Towards the end of his life he was Bapu or Bapuji to everyone who knew him.

In 1922, Gandhi launched a civil disobedience movement in Bardoli. But in Chauri Chaura, in the United Provinces, a mob went berserk, set fire to a police station and killed the policemen when they tried to escape. Gandhi promptly called off the movement. The other political leaders were unhappy with this decision. The government grabbed the opportunity and threw Gandhi into prison. When he came out of prison, he found the country deeply divided on religious lines. Hindu-Muslim enmity was rising and there were riots everywhere. In September 1924, Gandhi went on a fast for twenty-one days, for the cause of Hindu-Muslim brotherhood. On the twenty-first day, he listened to a Christian hymn, verses from the Koran, a Hindu hymn and chanting from the Upanishads. Then he broke his fast.

For the next five years, Gandhi distanced himself from the freedom struggle.

He believed that political freedom was worthless, unless it was accompanied by social and economic freedom. He was occupied with issues like Hindu-Muslim unity, the abolition of untouchability, the revival of hand weaving and spinning, the equality of women and the development of a village economy. He travelled the length and breadth of the country talking to people at mammoth meetings, and sometimes, just sitting in silence. The people sat silently with him, content simply to be in the presence of the Mahatma.

But in 1928, he was back in the political arena. He decided to launch another Satyagraha in Bardoli. The Satyagraha was conducted by Vallabhbhai Patel, who was then the mayor of Ahmedabad and a close associate of Gandhi. The government had increased taxes, and the villagers were to offer a non-violent protest. They refused to pay the taxes. For months, the peasants suffered their cattle to be seized, their possessions to be confiscated and their farms to be taken away. They courted arrest and went to jail. Through it all they stood their ground and remained non-violent. Finally the government capitulated. The prisoners were released, all confiscated property was returned and the rise in taxes was cancelled. The Satyagraha had succeeded.

In 1930, the Congress Working Committee decided to launch a nationwide civil disobedience movement, but it was left to Gandhi to decide when, where and how. All eyes, Indian and British, were on the little man in the loin cloth. Everyone wondered what he would do. In March 1930, Gandhi walked for twenty-four days to the seashore at Dandi, and picked up a handful of salt. Under the British law, this was an illegal act. It was the signal for all of India to participate in a massive movement of civil disobedience. Everywhere people took out processions or made salt at the sea, and were arrested in thousands. Jawaharlal Nehru, the President of the Congress, was thrown into prison. The jails, at one point, were filled with more than sixty thousand protestors. The British assaulted the Indians and tried to cow them down with brutality. But there were no reports of Indian violence anywhere, except at Chittagong, and there was no Congress violence at all. It was a triumph for the doctrine of Ahimsa.

Gandhi attended the Second Round Table Conference in London. On his return, in December 1931, he was imprisoned again. While in prison, he heard that the British government had granted a separate electorate to the "untouchables". Gandhi was anguished. He wanted the "Harijans", as he called them, to be integrated into the Hindu fold. A separate electorate would only deepen the division.

In September 1932, Gandhi went on a fast unto death. The effect of this fast was phenomenal. Thousands of temples all over India opened their gates to the "untouchables". Chaste Hindus sat down to eat with their "untouchable" brethren. If only for the sake of their Mahatma, Hindus, at least for the moment, set aside their practice of the iniquitous tradition. Ambedkar, the leader of the "untouchables", did not share Gandhi's optimistic view that Hindus would repent and eventually discontinue the practice of untouchability. Convinced that economic and social considerations would always outweigh the demands of humanitarian justice and compassion, he held that separate electorates were the only way to ensure the empowerment of his community. But finally, he came to a compromise with the Hindu leaders, and Gandhi ended his fast.

By 1942, the whole country was restive. The world was at war, but India was impatient for independence. Gandhi announced the Quit India movement. He was promptly imprisoned. Riots and violence broke out everywhere. Britain began to realize that Indian independence was inevitable. The next few years saw hectic negotiations for the transfer of power. But a wide chasm separated the Congress and the Muslim League. The Muslim League, led by Jinnah, did not want to share power – they wanted to create a separate nation for the Muslims.

By 1946, Hindu-Muslim riots were rampant everywhere. The most disturbing reports came from Noakhali in East Bengal. From November 1946 to March 1947, with a small band of volunteers, Gandhi toured the villages of East Bengal. For five months, the 77-year-old Bapu and his companions walked barefoot through hostile terrain, unmindful of the danger to their lives, trying to forge peace between Hindus and Muslims.

But Partition became inevitable. In August 1947, Pakistan and India were born, two nations created out of one. The Partition resulted in a bloodbath the likes of which history has never witnessed. Gandhi's reaction to the Two-Nation theory was one of bewilderment and incredulity. He described it as an untruth; in his dictionary there was no stronger word. Gandhi was inconsolable. "*Vivisect me before you vivisect India,*" was his anguished comment.

He went on a fast, until the delegates of various religious, ethnic and political groups took a pledge that they would not indulge in anti-Muslim violence. The mosques which had been wrested from the Muslims were returned to them. Muslims were allowed to go back to their homes, and were assured of protection. The Hindu extremists were incensed because they felt Gandhi was appeasing the Muslims and pandering to Pakistan.

On the 30th of January, 1948 Gandhi walked to the prayer ground at the Birla House in Delhi. About five hundred people had gathered for the daily prayer meeting. Many people came forward to greet him. A man broke out of the group and came towards Gandhi. He was Nathuram Godse, a Hindu extremist. Godse pushed Gandhi's companion away, and standing two feet away from the Mahatma, fired three shots from a small automatic pistol.

Bapu murmured, "Hey Ram," and fell to the ground. He died instantly.

"The light has gone out of our lives, and there is darkness everywhere," said Jawaharlal Nehru, the Indian Prime Minister. He reflected the mood of the entire nation.

The whole world mourned the death of an extraordinary man. He had shown the world the power of truth, humility and non-violence. He had turned ordinary men into heroes and martyrs.

In Bapu's death, the curtain fell upon a time and battle never before witnessed in human history. There have been many wars through many ages, but none fought with weapons so gentle, spirits so strong and forces so moral.

For trade and institutional requirements, please contact:

Karadi Tales Company Pvt. Ltd.
3A Dev Regency 11 First Main Road Gandhinagar Adyar Chennai 600020.
Ph: +9144 4205 4243 Fax: +9144 2440 3728
Email: contact@karaditales.com
Website: www.karaditales.com